Wee Scotch Whisky Tales by
Ian R Mitchell

ANGELS' SHARE

First published by

an imprint of
Neil Wilson Publishing Ltd
www.nwp.co.uk

A catalogue record for this book is available from the British Library.

ISBN: 978-1-906476-28-1
Ebook ISBN: 978-1-906000-79-0

Printed and bound in the EU

CONTENTS

Preface

LIKE MOST PEOPLE, my interest in whisky started with my drinking it and finding that it was the cure for all ills, physical and mental. As the years progressed my taste developed, as my means increased, from the firewater to which my purse initially stretched, towards an enjoyment of the finer pleasures of the myriad malts we are blessed with. A secondary gratification came in that I could then marry my profession as an historian with an interest in the plethora of tales associated with the amber dew, not just the stirring tales of the illicit distillers which add so much historical flavour to the story of out national drink, but also in exploring the connections of *uisge beatha* with the wider events of Scottish history – the Act of Union of 1707, the Highland Clearances and others. Hopefully this small collection of tales will interest the devoted tippler and inform him or her about some of the fascinating background to the emergence of whisky from the mists of time, and further that they will enjoy the tales as they should be, with a drap o' the *craitur* to hand.

Ian R Mitchell, Glasgow

1 Ferintosh: Sadly Lost?

'DUTY-FREE' WHISKY is something we have all been offered on air flights and in airport shopping malls; usually it is a product which has at best a small discount off the official High Street price, but occasionally it costs more to the unwary for a drap o' the *craitur* than a trip to the supermarket would. But for a century there was a duty-free whisky that was widely sold in Scotland and which for many years accounted for the bulk of legal whisky sales. Distilled on the Black Isle, Ferintosh may be 'Sadly Lost' as our national bard, Robert Burns, put it, but its memory should not be.

The first tax on whisky was levied by the Scottish Parliament in 1644, at 2s 8d (13p) per pint (which was one-third of a gallon) of *aqua vitae*. This provided almost no government revenue since personal domestic consumption was exempt from taxation, and the thousands of small or sma' stills which sold to a local market were impossible to police. The first mention of an actual distillery is in an Act of the Scottish parliament of 1690 which exempted the owner of the distillery at Ferintosh on the Black Isle, one Duncan Forbes of Culloden, from paying tax on his product, in return for an annual payment of 400 Scottish merks (about £20 sterling.) Given the low tax return on *aqua vitae* at this time parliament probably thought it had made a good deal, but they were to be proven way wrong by subsequent developments.

The Forbes' of Culloden were an old Whig family, originally from Aberdeenshire, who had bought the Culloden estate in about 1625 and then gradually extended their landholdings in the Moray Firth area, including the lands of Ferintosh. Strong adherents of the Protestant Succession, they had supported William and Mary in the Glorious Revolution of 1689-90 against the Catholic James II and VII and in the subsequent military conflicts. The lands and property of the Forbes' were then plundered and damaged by a force of 700 Jacobite insurgents when Forbes was off fighting elsewhere. Amongst other damages for which he claimed £45,000 compensation, he stated he had 'suffered the loss of his brewery of *aqua vitae* by fire in his absence.' Forbes was awarded a much smaller sum and given the tax exemption, supposedly in perpetuity, for what was probably the first legally established commercial whisky distillery in Scotland.

This exemption from tax which Ferintosh enjoyed survived the Act of Union of 1707. Whisky was still, pardon the expression, 'small beer' in the tax scheme of things and the new British Parliament was much more interested in extending the English tax system on ale north of the border, rather than bothering with what was still a very small-scale industry, as was then the production of *aqua vitae*. The Forbes' family's loyalty to the Hanoverian succession also survived the Union, and they were out with their retainers in the 1715 uprising opposing the Old Pretender, and then much more so in 1745 rebellion, when the Young Pretender landed.

Duncan Forbes of Culloden was at this latter time Lord Advocate of Scotland and had succeeded to the estate of his elder brother, known as 'Bumper' John who had basically drank himself to death. Forbes not only raised a militia to fight Bonnie Prince Charlie – which tied down many Jacobite troops in the north – but also persuaded many Highland chiefs to stay neutral in the conflict. Walter Scott later argued that Duncan Forbes did more than any man alive to save the Hanoverian dynasty. He nevertheless fell from favour with his efforts to promote leniency in the aftermath of the Rebellion and died in 1747.

But the Forbes' were still key players politically in what was then called North Britain, and another Jacobite rebellion was expected – hence the building of the massive Fort George on the Moray coast – and the Ferintosh tax exemption was continued. By the middle of the 18th century the growth in the popularity of whisky and whisky consumption meant that the Forbes family's earnings from Ferintosh, from being merely pocket money, had become a major part of their income. Estimates are impossible verify but it was said that Duncan Forbes had gained £18,000 a year from the profits of his tax-exempt whisky.[1] Whilst Forbes was off fighting the Jacobites, Culloden House was once again occupied – as it had been in 1689 – by supporters of the Stuarts, including no less than Bonnie Prince Charlie himself, who spent the nights before the Battle of Culloden there, and was reputed to have drunk a bottle of Ferintosh before bedtime.

Up until the 1770s, Ferintosh out-produced the other legal distilleries in Scotland – there were less than 10 of their number – both in volume and quality. In 1766 Ferintosh distilled 68,000 proof gallons while the total output from the other distilleries was 35,000 gallons. Duncan Forbes' son Arthur married an English heiress, as did so many Scottish lairds of the time, and moved south but he greatly expanded the operations at Ferintosh and there were reputedly four distilleries operating in the area under his ownership, with output peaking in the early 1780s at over 120,000 gallons of spirit annually. The wealth produced by this enabled Arthur to employ the Adam brothers in remodelling Culloden House into the Palladian mansion it remains today.

These distilleries were large-scale operations which employed, directly or indirectly over 1,000 people. However the Old Statistical Account of 1791-2 subsequently described a very different situation from the heyday of Ferintosh:

[1] Worth around £2.5m today.

4

There are buildings which during the existence of the Ferintosh privilege were erected by the company for the purpose of distilling and now lie unoccupied. They are of a very considerable extent ...

What had happened? In 1784 parliament ended the Ferintosh tax exemption, in return for a one-off payment of £21,000. This was admittedly a huge sum at that time, but when it is recalled that on the output of whisky the distillery had produced, Forbes of Culloden should have been paying – according to his numerous critics – £20,000 of tax anually, then the damage to his financial position is clear. One reason that this change happened was simply that whisky had become so popular that a tax exemption, which had originally been a cheap way of rewarding a political favourite, was now a gaping hole in the national revenue. The legislation cites this as a reason, for ending the privilege, and gave another:

Which exemption has been found detrimental to the Revenue and prejudicial to the distillery in other parts of Scotland.

The increasing popularity of whisky had transformed it in the Lowlands from a cottage industry to an increasingly industrial one. From the 1770s large-scale distillers like John Stein in Clackmannanshire were investing huge amounts of capital in producing whisky, and they resented the tax exemption given to Ferintosh which in turn forced them to produce a cheaper, lower quality product in order to compete on price. This increasingly powerful group of industrial capitalists were becoming more important to the government than the maintenance of goodwill to a landed family whose favours were all in the past, and which was of decreasing political importance now that the Jacobite threat had clearly died. It is no accident that the Ferintosh privilege was ended at the same time as the ban on Highland dress, the bagpipes and the Gaelic language. Times had changed.

In *The Making of Scotch Whisky* by JR Hume and Michael S Moss (1981) – from which the figures in this article are taken – the authors state that 'the name (Ferintosh) became synonymous with good quality spirit' in the 18th century, as its popularity testified. It has the distinction of having had panegyrics composed to it in two languages, Scots and Gaelic. People are familiar with Burns' lament on the demise of Ferintosh.

> *Thee, Ferintosh, O sadly lost*
> *Scotland lament frae coast tae coast*
> *Now colic grips and barkin' hoast*
> *May kill us a'*

But sometime before that, in his poem *Moladh an Uisge-Beatha* (In Praise of Whisky) the poet Uilleam (William) Ross had written of the virtues of Ferintosh as follows:

Stuth glan Toiseachd gun truailleadh ...
'S cha b'e druaip na Frainge

Which roughly translates as:

Clean drink of Ferintosh without impurities ...
None of your rubbish from France.

Although it was considered to taste better than the Lowland competition it is probably a mistake to see Ferintosh as a Highland single malt, as we might drink today. Adam Smith in his *Wealth of Nations* in 1776 stated that whisky was generally made from one-third malted barley and a mixture of other grains, malted and unmalted. There is a contract from 1757 between Forbes of Culloden and one Donald MacDonald for 25 gallons of *aqua vitae,* 'being Spirits distilled from Corn of the growth of the Lands of Ferintosh.' The probable sites of the various distilleries operated by the Forbes family in the vicinity of Ryefield House on the Black Isle were excavated by the North of Scotland Archeological Society in 2009-10, and the largest of these at Mulchaich consisted of seven large, dressed-stone buildings, some three stories high, indicating a considerable undertaking. Interestingly one of the buildings would appear to have been a corn-drying kiln, indicating that that grain, possibly in addition to barley, was used widely in the distillation of Ferintosh.

The reputation of the whisky was such that, even after it ceased production, several others used the name to promote their product, most notably the Ben Wyvis Distillery of Dingwall which operated from 1879 till 1926. And then the name Ferintosh was, like the whisky, sadly lost ... or was it? In the last decade or so a new strain of *lactobacillus* has been identified in the whisky production process and it has been given, by some biochemist with a knowledge of whisky-distilling history, the designation ... *lactobacillus ferintoshensis*. There are microbreweries on the Black Isle today, maybe one day we will have a boutique distillery producing a dram which revives the Ferintosh name?

2 A Riot Creates The Whisky Island

WHEN SCOTLAND AND England unified their parliaments in 1707, there was very little of what we would now call 'whisky' distilled in Scotland, apart from in scattered sma' stills. The only major producer was the aforementioned Forbes of Culloden's distillery at Ferintosh, where he was allowed to produce his *aqua vitae* tax-free and appears to have used a lot of corn in the production process as I outlined in the previous chapter. The national drinks were claret and wine for the upper classes, and tippeny ale for the lower orders; almost all malted grains were used for brewing, rather than for distillation, at that time. A convoluted process, in which malted barley was a key player, was to change this situation completely and establish whisky as Scotland's 'national drink'.

The Union was not popular in its early years, to say the least. Jacobites opposed it because it blocked the way to the return of the Stuarts, Presbyterians opposed it as it introduced toleration for non-Presbyterians in 1712 and most importantly, as a move to equalise Scottish and English taxes a malt tax was proposed in 1713 which was so unpopular that it contributed to a motion in parliament to repeal the Act of Union itself. This motion narrowly failed – and the imposition of the tax itself was postponed. However, in 1725 the London government came back with its malt tax proposal, though at a lower rate of 3d a barrel of beer brewed in Scotland against the English rate which was double that. Opposition to the tax amongst the populace was general, leading to a brewers' strike in Edinburgh, and riots throughout the land, but nowhere was hostility more widespread than in Glasgow.

In June 1725 crowds assembled in the centre of the city and rang the town's fire bell to summon forth support. Initially they molested the excisemen sent to collect the new tax, but then turned their attention to the local MP, Daniel (or Donald) Campbell, who was reputed – correctly – to have voted for the malt tax. Campbell was an exceedingly rich merchant capitalist who had in 1711-12 built the Shawfield Mansion in the centre of Glasgow, at the junction of the Trongate and Glassford Street. This was then the finest Palladian mansion in the city and possibly in Scotland. The crowd smashed the windows of the mansion and looted many of its contents.

The authorities called in the military to restore order, and Lord Deloriane's Foot, commanded by one Captain Bushell, fired on the demonstrators, killing nine and wounding 16 of them – without having first read the Riot Act or having fired warning shots, as was legally required. This failed to restore order and the Glasgow magistrates ordered the troops to leave the city, subsequently charging Bushell with murder – a charge eventually dropped. The troops retreated towards Dumbarton Castle and were again attacked. Again they fired and again killed an undetermined further number of rioters. Finally General Wade, commander-in-chief of forces in Scotland, was sent to Glasgow with a much larger number of troops, including the Earl of Stair's Dragoons, to quell the rioting. Wade was accompanied by the Lord Advocate, Duncan Forbes of Culloden (of untaxed Ferintosh fame covered in Chapter 1!) who exacted retribution for the riots. Several of the culprits were jailed, fined, whipped through the town or exiled for life.

Forbes also arrested Provost Millar and the rest of the town council for alleged complicity with the rioters. Though these charges were subsequently dropped the council was fined a total of almost £10,000 to cover the cost of the riots and was forced to sell off most of the city's common lands to pay the fine. Much of the compensation went direct to Campbell of Shawfield, a total of more than £6,000 for his damages. However this can be seen as a reward for a loyal government supporter rather than valid compensation, as two separate estimates by tradesmen for repairs to the building (which was not demolished or burnt down as many stories state) came to a few hundred rather than thousands of pounds. Until its demolition in 1792

Shawfield Mansion remained the most luxurious dwelling in the city – so much so that Bonnie Prince Charlie stayed there in 1746 during his retreat to Culloden and fell for the charms of Clementina Walkinshaw. (Whilst he did so, Campbell of Shawfield, who had fled Glasgow, raised at his own expense a militia to fight the Jacobite army).

But to return to our story, one effect of the malt tax led to a decline in ale drinking in Scotland and an increased consumption of whisky – much of it produced from the illicit sma' stills in the Highlands and smuggled south. 'Whisky' at this time was a term which covered a multitude of sins, and included any distillation made from any malted grain – or grain mixed with unmalted grain – and flavoured with herbs, raisins, spices and a variety of other ingredients to make it palatable. The emergence of a drink based on malted barley took longer to emerge, and again has a connection with our story of the malt tax.

With his fairly ill-gotten gains from the Shawfield Riots, Daniel Campbell procured the bulk of the purchase price for the island of Islay in the Inner Hebrides. He set about the process of agricultural improvement on the island, developing mining and other enterprises as well as introducing new methods of crop rotation and new crops, such as the higher yielding barley to replace the strain called 'bere'. This led to the situation where tenant farmers who had a surplus of the grain could use it to produce the drink that was to become known as whisky. That this practice had become widespread in the 50 years after Campbell bought Islay is shown by the comments of the Revd Archibald Robertson of Kildalton parish in 1777:

We have not an excise officer in the whole island. The quantity therefore of whisky made here is very great; and the evil, that follows drinking to excess of this liquor, is very visible in this island.

Initially these were sma' stills bubbling away for personal or local consumption, with a little smuggling sideline to the Lowlands. The Highland product, made from malted barley was considered to taste much better than Lowland whisky, generally made with other grains, and was in increasing demand. And by 1750 it was this drink that was generally known as whisky, and the term did not any longer apply to the rougher grain spirits flavoured like cordials.

At the same time another development took place which was of great importance and can be regarded as the first step towards making Islay – arguably – the malt whisky capital of the world. Campbell of Shawfield had died in 1753 and his estate had passed to his grandson, who carried on the process of economic development, most notably with the construction of the planned village of Bowmore in the 1760s. The new laird encouraged one Daniel Simson, a farmer at Bridgend who had done some small-scale distilling, to open a larger enterprise in the town, and – probably some time before 1779 – Bowmore Distillery opened. This was the first of a long and illustrious line which, after the Excise Act of 1823, basically doomed the sma' stills and paved the way for large-scale distilleries; by the mid-19th century nine such distilleries were operating on the island.

However, the illicit tradition continued for many years afterwards. 'Baldy Cladach' was tenant of a remote croft at Cladach on the east coast of Islay, accessible only by a lengthy track from Ballygrant. A strong man, he was famed for being able to carry his own weight in sacked grain to Cladach from Ballygrant. The suspicious excisemen investigated and he was duly evicted from his holding, emigrating to Canada around 1850. Alhough his still was destroyed, his store of whisky was not and it is rumoured to be out there awaiting discovery yet.

By a circuitous route, the tax on the malt in beer had contributed to the eventual emergence of malt whisky. The rest, as they say, is history. It is also interesting that until the development of North Sea oil, the present-day opponents of the Union of 1707 were wont to argue that Scotland could be economically viable on the tax revenue – not of black oil but of the golden spirit. The tax receipts from Islay whisky alone are estimated at £500,000,000 annually. And it is further interesting – and reassuring – to note that, while the oil will not last forever, the whisky will.

3 The Whisky Wars in Scotland

THE PHRASE 'ILLICIT distilling' conjures up a picture of a Highland crofter, sitting patiently at his sma' still, producing a modest drop of *usquebae* for friends and neighbours. And for the last two centuries that has been the basic reality of contraband whisky. But for almost a century before that, illicit whisky production was one of Scotland's largest industries, and it was based far more in the North-east of Scotland, than in the Highlands. This is the almost forgotten period of the Whisky Wars, which raged from the middle of the 18th century until the 1820s. Ultimately it took the military resources of the British state, and a long, low-level counter-insurgency operation, to bring the Whisky Wars to an end.

The illicit whisky trade during this period spread like wildfire in the north-eastern upland plateau between the Highlands and the available markets in the Lowlands. By the 1780s it was estimated that 90% of all Scottish whisky sales were illicit, and an observer commented that the trade had 'spread over the whole face of the country, where the face of an Exciseman is never seen'. There were over 200 active stills in Glenlivet in about 1800, and Tomintoul was described 15 years later as 'a wild mountain village, where drinking, dancing and swearing went on all the time'. The Cabrach, to the east of Glenlivet, was another lawless area, again with a couple of hundred active stills. There was no comparable mass production in the Highland areas proper.

Suppressing the trade was especially difficult because many landlords connived with it, since the money it brought in ensured that their tenants could pay their rents, otherwise a difficulty due to the low crop yields of these marginal lands. Barley made into whisky was estimated to produce between five to ten times its economic yield as a food crop. In some kirks of the North-east at this time a portion of the gallery was known as the 'smugglers' loft', where they would sit holding their heads high because they could easily pay their pew rent – and their farms rents as well.

THE BACKGROUND

Whisky has been distilled in Scotland from probably the 15th century, but by the middle of the 18th it had become the national drink. Distilleries had to be licensed by the state, and most of these legal distilleries were fairly large-scale. By law they had to have a minimum still capacity of 500 gallons. The problem was that after the Union, as a price for access to English colonial markets, Scots had to accept a share of England's tax burden – a bargain which the Scots found unreasonable. As mentioned in Chapter 2, the imposition of malt tax caused the most resentment.

The malt tax, along with the high excise duty (which it was suspected was to protect English gin producers) on the spirit itself, meant that large distilleries which were open to excise inspection were at a major disadvantage, compared with small law-breaking distillers in remote areas who avoided all taxation. John Stein, a Lowland distiller, stated in 1797 that 'owing to the interference of Highland spirits, we have been unable to find sales'. Stein and other large-scale distillers like the Haig family were paying seven shillings a gallon excise on their product and could not compete with the sma' stills that were paying nothing.

For Robert Burns and many other Scots, whisky went not only with freedom, but with good health. One excise-man agreed with Burns, noting in 1786 that 'the ruddy complexion and strength of these people is not owing to water-drinking, but to the *aqua vitae*.' It should also be mentioned that until well into the 19th century, and even afterwards in country districts, whisky was the only painkiller available to most of the common people, who could ill-afford the legal but expensive opiates at the time. One doctor is recorded as asking a countryman what happened if any of his family were ill.

'We drink fusky' was the reply.
'And if you don't get better?'
'We drink mair fusky.'
'And if you still don't get better?'
'We dee.'

ORGANISATION OF THE TRADE

The illicit whisky smuggling trade was highly organised, and often ingenious methods were used. Women walking with their wares to market in neighbouring towns would acquire miraculous pregnancies – inflated bladders full of the whisky which they would deliver or sell to customers. Innocent-looking parties on coffin tracks, walking to the cemetery and resting awhile from the labour of carrying their burden, might well be over-refreshed – not from drowning their sorrows at the loss of the supposed deceased, but because the coffin held supplies of whisky for delivery to consumers.

But the main method of delivery of illicit whisky was a well-organised armed convoy. Once the amber dew had been distilled, it was poured into barrels (called 'akers') and these were set on panniers over a pony, which generally carried four five-gallon barrels. A long string of ponies was tied together, and the animals proceeded to walk, accompanied by 20 or 30 men, on the outward journey to their destination – then the men would ride back home on the empty animals. Accounts speak of how heavily armed the smugglers were, carrying cudgels, swords and pistols. The whisky convoy was accompanied by dogs, which would have been excellent as lookouts, picking up the sound and scent of any unwelcome persons along the way. The journey from the Cabrach or Glenlivet to the Mearns, Strathmore or the

Laigh o' Moray, was one that occupied two or three days' or (as often as not) nights' walking for the smugglers. Stealth was at least as important for the smugglers as speed, and they utilised the little-frequented whisky roads through and over the mountains.

One 'Whisky Road' started in the Braes o' Glenlivet and went over the Ladder Hills by Ladderfoot, thence descending to Bellabeg on Donside. From Bellabeg the convoy would then have moved, by night, through the populated district of Cromar, before arriving at Aboyne and starting the next stage of their journey over the Fungle Road the following day. Formerly called the Cattrin Road, named from its reiver (catteran) days, this was an established drove road which the smugglers followed over the hill to Tarfside in Glenesk.

Thereafter, the law-abiding drovers followed the North Esk to Fettercairn and then to market. But the smugglers walked their ponies another route south, through the less-frequented Clash of Wirren to Glen Lethnot, and then south by Bridgend to the track which went between the Brown and White Caterthuns (Iron Age hill-forts), from which vantage point (and splendid camp) they waited for night to fall, to descend upon Brechin. A place thereabouts is called 'Donald's Bed', where a murdered exciseman lay for 20 years before discovery – showing that at least one of the law-enforcers number had been, regrettably, wise to the smugglers' secret route.

THE DE'IL TAK THE EXCISEMAN

Whatever problems they encountered on the 'Whisky Roads', the smugglers knew none that compared with the terrors of the gauger, or exciseman. After the '45, soldiers were stationed at places like Braemar and Corgarff castles, as a counter-insurgency measure against an expected further Jacobite rising. However, once the residual Jacobites were hunted down the soldiery became primarily involved in excise duties, aiding the excisemen in their thankless struggles. The gauger's was an unpopular and dangerous job, and it is not surprising that many excisemen took the easy option and turned a blind eye to smuggling. However, professional pride and the bounties attendant upon seizure of contraband, provoked many into actions of incredible heroism.

But the battles were not always won by the gaugers, as is recorded in the ballad *The Battle of Corrymuckloch*, which describes an encounter that took place around 1820 between some smugglers and excisemen supported by soldiers of the Royal Scots Greys. The contraband had come to Glen Quoich in Perthshire when the smugglers were accosted by the armed soldiery. Using sticks – and stones from a dyke for missiles – they put the soldiers ('the beardies') to flight and captured the exciseman. The poem makes clear that the soldiers were equipped with firearms, but also that they declined to use them when faced with resolute opposition, indicating perhaps a certain lack of enthusiasm for their task.

Then Donald and his men drew up and Donald gied command
And aa the arms poor Donald had was a stick in ilka hand
An when poor Donald's men drew up a guid stane dyke was at their back
Sae when their sticks tae prunach went, wi stanes they made attack. [2]

But Donald and his men stuck fast an garr'd the beardies quit the field
The gauger he was thumped weel afore his pride would lat him yield
Then Donald's men they aa cried oot, 'Ye nasty filthy gauger loon
If ye come back ye'll ne'er win haim, tae see yer Ouchterarder Toon.'

Sometimes the gaugers simply, and wisely, declined combat. The Revd Thomas Guthrie wrote that as a boy in Brechin in the early years of the 19th century, the sight of men 'come down from the wilds of Aberdeenshire or the glens of the Grampians' to sell their whisky was a common sight, carrying it on 'small, shaggy but brave and hardy steeds'. He confirms that they watched 'on some commanding eminence' (probably one of the Caterthuns) during the day, and only moved onto the plains at night, distributing their whisky 'to agents they had everywhere'. And for the smugglers, there was nothing like rubbing the outnumbered and defeated enemy's nose in the dirt, as Guthrie noted:

I have seen a troop of thirty of them riding in Indian file, and in broad day, though the streets of Brechin, after they had succeeded in disposing of their whisky, and they rode leisurely along, beating time with their formidable cudgels on the empty barrels to the great

[2] *prunach* = splintered.

amusement of the public and the mortification of the excisemen,
who had nothing for it but to bite their nails and stand, as best they
could, the raillery of the smugglers and the laughter of the people.

THE END OF THE TRADE

The local lairds' connivance with smuggling was shown by
the low penalties imposed in areas where illicit distilling was
endemic: while the fine in Fife or Ayr was the statutory £20,
at Aberdeen (where the legal officials were often also local
landowners) capture and conviction would cost you on
average 11s 3d. One JP in a north-east court was embar-
rassed when the accused said to him, 'I havnae made a drap
since yon wee keg I sent tae yersel.' Fines were often paid by
the smuggling community through a levy, and thus did not
drive the illicit distiller out of business.

Eventually the government was compelled to deal rigor-
ously with a trade which resulted in so much lost revenue.
By 1822 agents for the excise were assisting at all civil trials,
ensuring that the minimum penalty of a £20 fine or six
months in prison was imposed, with transportation to Van
Diemen's Land for those who violently resisted arrest. The
increased success of the militarily-backed seizures (the end
of the Napoleonic War in 1815 had released large numbers
of soldiers for this duty) prove the point. In 1822 alone
there were almost 10,000 people prosecuted for breaking
the excise laws in the Aberdeen and Elgin courts alone,
amounting to over two-thirds of total Scottish prosecutions

– emphasising again the key role of the North-east in the history of illicit distilling. But increased repression would not have worked without economic measures to back it up.

The duty on whisky was massively reduced to 2s 3d per gallon, giving the advantage back to licensed distillers with their economies of scale. In addition, tenants found guilty of illicit distilling were evicted by local landowners, some of whom turned to distilling themselves – or more commonly they leased or sold land to legal distilling operations. By 1832 less than 200 cases concerning illicit distilling were heard in Scottish courts. 'Poachers', like John Begg on Deeside and George Smith in Glenlivet, had by then turned 'gamekeepers' and set up commercial production. They did this in the face of local hostility; for many years Smith went around armed and in fear of attack. The new status of whisky was demonstrated by the presentation of a bottle of Glenlivet (albeit illicit) by Sir Walter Scott to King George IV on his visit to Edinburgh in 1822. The beginning of the end of the illicit distilling industry in 1823 contributed, however, to massive depopulation on upper Donside, the Cabrach and in Glenlivet, a little recorded exodus as it was mostly voluntary rather than enforced. The 'Whisky Wars' were over.

The trade thereafter survived only in really remote Highland locations. James Mitchell records that as he was taking a drive up Glen Moriston in the 1840s, 'I saw before me at some little distance about twenty five Highland horses tied to each other, and carrying two kegs of whisky each'. The men walking with the ponies were in bonnets and plaids, carrying bludgeons. They recognised Mitchell and, instead of beating him, offered him a dram. Such folkloric relics were, however, small beer to the days when large areas of north-east Scotland in particular were in a state of armed conflict between the distillers and gaugers in the scarce-remembered 'Whisky Wars'.

4 The Strathdon Dram: The One That Got Away

SPEYSIDE WHISKY IS world-renowned. And few have not heard of the Royal Lochnagar Distillery on Deeside. But between the Spey and the Dee, those two major rivers of north-east Scotland lies a more modest watercourse, the River Don. Donside attracts little tourism, which is a pity as it is a beautiful and fascinating area of castles, rolling hills, and legends. Especially whisky legends.

The Don no longer produces whisky, but it once did. The fertile reaches of Upper Donside (Strathdon) were for many years bandit country, where hundreds of sma' stills were concealed in the surrounding hillsides. The pot still, fondly named the 'Yowie wi the crookit horn' (*Anglice* 'ewe with the crooked horn') brought a brief prosperity to Strathdon in the 75 years following the Jacobite Rebellion of 1745.

Upper Donside had been Jacobite territory and Corgarff Castle was garrisoned by Hanoverian troops after the '45. These troops were very successful in stamping out the last relics of Jacobitism. But they were much less successful in stamping out the ensuing phenomenon that lengthened their stay, illicit whisky distilling.

In the years following the Jacobite defeat, the sma' stills spread across the land. Looking back on this period in 1845, the Minister of the Kirk of Scotland at Strathdon stated:

This parish was one of the strongholds of smuggling. The inhabitants of Corgarff, the glens, and not a few of the lower part of the parish were professed smugglers. The Revenue officers were set at defiance. To be engaged in illicit distillation was neither looked upon as a crime, nor considered a disgrace.

His comment makes it clear that this period was well over by 1845. The Kirk itself was an opponent of whisky smuggling, though religious opposition was not the cause of the trade's ultimate demise.

Defiance was indeed the watchword. And in the upper reaches of lonely Glen Noughty (or Nochty), a side-glen off Strathdon, stands today, and is marked on the OS map, a ruin called *Duffdefiance*. A man had been evicted from Glenlivet for illicit distilling. Unabashed, he crossed the Ladder Hills to Donside, and established a new distilling site in Glen Nochty. Here he also gained squatter's rights by having a house built with its 'lum reeking' before being challenged by the local laird, one Duff – *aka* the Earl of Fife. Hence, *Duffdefiance*. In my opinion the building marked as being Duffdefiance on the map is a later construction; nearer the burn lies the remains of a cruder building which is more likely to have provided the distiller's abode.

In Glen Nochty also took place a conflict, the Battle of Glen Nochty, between distillers and excisemen that led to a popular ballad being written about it. Interestingly this ballad is written to the tune of the Jacobite song, *Johnny Cope*. A Glenlivet man, John Milne, wrote the song, *Noughty Glens*, and gave the honours to his compatriots against the reputedly cowardly Donside men. The ballad has 64 verses and was published in 1826, shortly after the events it describes. The song launched Milne as an itinerant poet and songsheet seller, which was just as well, since his wife's whisky business was soon closed down. The poem starts with the excise officer, one McBain, leading his men into the glen:

We'll make them submit unto our will
We'll burn their bothies in the hill
We'll seize their whisky, every gill
Among Noughty glens in the morning

Glen Noughty lads they staid at hame
For fear that they should get the blame
But Glenlivet men they thought no shame
For to keep their ground in the morning.

So they gave him a dreadful fire
Which made his troops almost retire
Said he, Their courage I admire
Among Noughty glens in the morning

The Preventive commander said, 'We'll retire [3]
We cannot longer stand their fire
Though it be sore against my desire
To leave their glens in the morning.'

[3] Preventive commander = gauger

27

'You are the lads we dare not mock
We find them firm as any rock.'
So they ran like a fudgie cock [4]
And left their glens in the morning.

A fusillade drove the gaugers off, but they returned with soldiers from the Corgarff Castle garrison. They appear to have had little appetite for their work and when met with a hail of stones, also retreated. But though they won this battle the smugglers were soon to lose the war.

Apart from the attentions of the soldiers at Corgarff, other pressures were being brought to bear on the sma' still operators. Charles Forbes bought the estate which included much of Upper Donside and announce his intention to stamp out the trade. In 1825 he inserted clauses in all his tenants' leases, which stated that

> *He prohibits his tenants from all concern, directly or indirectly, in illicit malting and distillation, or the selling of spirits ... And he declares that a breach of this prohibition shall infer an immediate forfeiture of the lease.*

This had much more effect that the threat of arrest, usually accompanied by a small fine, in helping suppress the whisky trade. The song, *Noughty Glens*, mentioned above, sadly reflects this development:

[4] Fudgie = cowardly

But our gentlemen surveyed the hills
And sore destroyed the smuggling stills
Made their tenants submit to their wills
Among Noughty glens in the morning.

The family of McHardy, or rather the families, for there were many of them in Strathdon, had long been associated with illicit stills on Upper Donside, especially the McHardy's of Burnside and Corryhoul. The estate records of Forbes note that:

> *Margaret, widow of John McHardy of Easter Corryhoul, rents a farm at £13 a year, she has nine children and wishes to be continued a tenant, she has brewed whisky and has several times been fined.*

In spite of his prohibition against distilling and threat to evict culprits, the estate records note *'Agreed'* to her continued tenancy. Evicting a widow with nine children was probably a step too far even for Forbes.

The taxation burden on legal, large-scale distilling had been greatly reduced in 1823 and changes to revenue laws made it much easier for those with some capital to set up in legal business. It is rather thus ironic that the first legal distillery on Upper Donside was established by one James McHardy in Corgarff in 1826. McHardy possibly had fears about the security of his enterprise, since he set it up in the actual kitchens of Corgarff Castle where his potential customers included the local garrison. In the castle, and behind the secure star-shaped curtain wall, he probably felt he could survive local resentment. Today one can visit Corgarff Castle and see a fascinating reconstruction of McHardy's distillery. It is a reconstruction because the original legal distillery was attacked and burned to the ground when the soldiers were out on patrol. (Corgarff Castle is open all year, weekends only in winter. A beautiful building in a gorgeous location, and full of historical interest. Tel: 01975 651 460. www.historic-scotland.gov.uk.)

The destruction of the legal distillery had the authorities thirsting for revenge, or justice as they might call it. The *Aberdeen Journal* of 29th November 1826 carried the following statement:

REWARD
Whitehall, November 3rd 1826

Whereas it hath been humbly represented unto the King, that early on the morning of Monday, the 17th day of July last, a legal distillery at Corgarff Castle, in the parish of Strathdon in the Highlands of Aberdeenshire, was wilfully set on fire and destroyed, HIS MAJESTY is pleased to offer His most gracious pardon to any one of them, who shall discover his Accomplice or Accomplices therein.

Signed Robert Peel,
Excise Office, Edinburgh 7th November 1826.

And as for further encouragement, a Reward of ONE HUN-DRED POUNDS Is hereby offered to any person (except as afore-

*said) who shall discover the said Offender or Offenders, so that He,
She or They, may be apprehended and convicted of the said offence.
The said Reward to be paid on Conviction by the Commissioners
of His Majesty's Excise*

Geo. Pape, sec.

There was evidently a widespread involvement in the attack, and a local conspiracy of silence. Despite intensive investigations and the promise a pardon for culprits turning king's evidence – and also the offer of large reward of £100 – no one was ever convicted of the offence. One man, a certain Farquharson was apprehended for questioning by the excise officer, Mr Yates, but a mob confronted Yates, assaulted him and freed the suspect. The locals had successfully, for a time, destroyed a competitive threat to their illicit incomes. Gradually however, the illegal trade was reduced, though never completely eradicated, as an incident from much later in the 19th century showed.

Customs officers had come off the train at Ballater on Deeside and were preparing to head over the hills for Donside and catch the McHardys at their work. They were, however, overheard by a fellow McHardy on the platform, and he ran by a more direct route than that taken by the gaugers, to warn those at Burnside. When the officers arrived they met a man coming off the hill with a cartload of peats, but could find no still. It was under the load of peats. The still was probably re-assembled afterwards, but by this time whisky-making was an exciting hobby rather than the major source of income for local people. The railway line came to Ballater in 1864, so the story must refer to an occasion after that date.

The site of the McHardy illicit bothy is still there, a rickle of stones by the Corriehoul Burn above Burnside. It is set in a hollow by a stand of juniper which was the distillers' favourite fuel as it gave little smoke. Illicit distilling died out on Donside, and legal distilling never became established after the burning down of the Corgarff Castle distillery. That act probably ensured that there would never be a Strathdon Malt to rival the Glenlivet, or Lochnagar. We don't have the whisky, but we have the whisky legends.

5 The Deil's Awa Wi' Th'Exciseman: The Case of Malcolm Gillespie

THE EXCISEMAN, OR 'gauger' as he was known in the Scots vernacular, was probably the most hated figure in Scotland 200 years ago. This dislike was given a humorous slant in our national bard Robert Burns' poem, *The Exciseman*. Here the despised figure is carried off to Hell by the Devil (Auld Mahoun):

The deil cam fiddlin' through the toun,
And danced awa wi' th'Exciseman
And ilka wife cries 'Auld Mahoun,
I wish ye luck of the prize, man.'

Ironically Burns himself served a spell as an exciseman, though in the relatively quiet Dumfries area of south-west Scotland. His job would have been very different had he found himself in his forebears' homeland of north-east Scotland, where smuggling was rife and the conflict between distillers and gaugers became a low-level civil war, with fatalities on each side.

In the wild areas which lay between the Lowlands of the North-east and the Highlands proper, that is, the upland areas of the Cabrach, Glenlivet and Deeside, the illicit whisky industry was a massive enterprise. Here people did not just distil the *craitur* for the resulting conviviality, on the contrary most of their production was exported to the Lowland towns and cities. The money from the sale of the contraband did what farming in these poor areas could never do; it raised the money to pay the tenants' rent and left a good surplus for a decent living. Everyone, involved in the distilling or not, conspired to defeat the forces of the law. Local landlords, acting as Justices of the Peace, enforced ludicrously low fines on distillers – since these landlords too were often the recipients of the cash, as rent, from the ill-gotten gains of the distillers. Even the stationing of soldiers at Braemar and Corgarff castles, did little to halt the trade. That job fell to the gaugers.

The gauger was spurred on by the promise of a large bounty, given as a percentage of the value of the spirits seized. This was certainly a motivation in the case of the most successful of the excisemen, Malcolm Gillespie. The 'King of the Gaugers' Gillespie enjoyed a lavish lifestyle on the proceeds of his enormous seizures. But sheer love of adventure and excitement clearly motivated Gillespie, who had been turned down for a commission in the army since he could not afford to buy the officer's post – as was the procedure at that time. A native of Dunblane, Gillespie moved to the North-east around 1800, where his consider-able courage and talents were employed in suppressing the illicit whisky trade. While the soldiers in the mountains had little success in stamping out the supply side of the industry, located in well-hidden illicit stills, Gillespie concentrated, with much more success, in intercepting the contraband on its actual way to the lowland markets.

For over a quarter of a century Gillespie harassed the smugglers of Aberdeenshire. In that time he impounded 6535 gallons of whisky, 407 stills, 165 horses, 85 carts and 62,400 gallons of barley wash. Gillespie trained bulldogs to tumble the ponies carrying the akers of whisky, by biting their noses, and causing the spillage of their cargo. His own favourite dog suffered maryrdom by being shot dead by a smuggler. The ponies too suffered casualties. On one occasion Gillespie had been worsted by a superior number of foes, but as they fled, he shot the pony carrying their wares dead and prevented them triumphing. Gillespie and his men were armed with swords and pistols, which they unfailingly used. He himself sustained 42 wounds in his career and was battered near to death on frequent occasions.

Some of Gillespie's exploits are the stuff of legend. A party of smugglers set out from Upper Deeside in one instance, with ten cartloads of whisky and a numerous armed guard. It was night, and a fearful one, so the smugglers expected no exciseman to be abroad. They reached Culter outside Aberdeen without opposition, but here the gaugers lay in ambush, and a battle ensued between the two sides. In the end the smugglers fled, leaving several wounded and one of their men dead, and the whisky fell into Gillespie's hands.

We are lucky to have an account of Gillespie's exploits written in his own hand. One of the incidents it describes is the Battle of Inverurie in 1824, where a cavalcade of smugglers were intercepted heading for Aberdeen. Gillespie and a sole assistant stumbled on the 25 smugglers and their cargo, while the rest of the excisemen were scattered around. Gillespie describes the ensuing battle in his own words, using the third person:

> *This formidable group were very indifferent to his threats, and looked upon him with his assistant in a scornful way, and were proceeding onwards, when he immediately fired and killed a horse. The next shot he discharged went through the shoulder of a robust delinquent, in the very act of bringing down on Mr. Gillespie's head a large bludgeon. The whole gang were now upon Mr. G., but by this time the rest of his party had assembled and a terrible conflict ensued. Bloody heads, hats rolling on the ground, the reports of firing and other noise resembled the Battle of Waterloo, but in the end the lawless desperadoes were obliged to lay down their arms and submit to the laws of their country. Mr. G and his party were all much debilitated by severe wounds and bruises and loss of blood; but the greater part of the smugglers were in a much worse situation.*

Gillespie wrote this account of his work, glowing with professional pride, whilst in prison in 1827 awaiting trial for printing and circulating forged bills. This was then a capital offence, and he was convicted, and hanged in November

1827. Gillespie had probably hoped that an account of his loyal service to the state would result in a pardon, but it was not to be. Gillespie was a victim of his own efficiency, and the general success of the government's policy of suppressing the illicit whisky trade. This meant that prosecutions for illicit distilling in Scotland fell from 3,000 a year in 1823 to less than 300 in 1827. And so too fell the exciseman's bounties for seizure of the contraband. Gillespie, used to a generous income, turned to forgery to replace his declining bounties. It still seems harsh that a state which he had served so well, and so bravely, should in the end mete out to him a more severe punishment than was ever inflicted on any of the smugglers he caught. But all those smugglers he had had incarcerated, fined or simply forced into unwilling retirement, must have gloatingly echoed Burns' words as Gillespie was hanged.

We'll makk our maut, we'll brew our drink
We'll dance, and sing, and rejoice, man;
And mony braw thanks to the meikle black deil
That danced awa wi' th'Exciseman.

6 The National Bard and The National Dram

SHORTLY AFTER HIS death in 1796 Robert Burns emerged as the undisputed National Bard of Scotland. The foundation of the first Burns Club took place in 1801. This was the Greenock Burns Club, later known as the Mither Club. As such clubs spread, Burns' Suppers soon became a national event (at least in Lowland Scotland) on *Burns Nicht*, held on the anniversary of the poet's birthday, the 25th of January. Some decades previously, whisky had emerged as the national dram of Scotland. Though it had been distilled for several centuries, it had taken much longer for whisky to gain that pre-eminent affection in Scotland quickly achieved by Burns.

For centuries the preferred drink of the upper classes was claret, and that of the poor 'tippenny', a cheap ale – but over the course of the 18th century whisky gradually emerged as the favoured alcoholic beverage in the country. This is reflected in Burns' poetry, where his praise of the craitur out-matches his praise of any other form of alcohol. Indeed, at a Burns Supper anywhere in the world, it would be unthinkable to toast the haggis with anything other than whisky, the poet's favourite beverage.

Few, if any, poets have sung the praises of whisky as did

Robert Burns. Just as he had claimed that many Scots virtues – such as martial valour – stemmed from the consumption of the national dish, the humble haggis, so Rabbie attributed several benefits to the consumption of whisky. The first of these was good health.

In his poem *Scottish Drink*, Burns argues that good health is one of the benefits of whisky drinking, especially as a preventative against colic and 'barkin' hoast. The poet also prescribes a dram or two as a cure for writers' block.

> *O Whisky! Soul o' plays and pranks!*
> *Accept a Bardie's grateful thanks!*
> *When wanting thee, what tuneless cranks*
> *Are my poor verses!*
> *Thou comes – they rattle I' the ranks*
> *At ither's airses!*

– and elsewhere he wrote of the 'muse-inspirin' aqua-vitae.' In *The Author's Earnest Cry and Prayer* Burns writes probably his most famous line on the subject of the national dram – *Freedom and whisky gang thegither*. Oft quoted, but who knows the context and hence the true meaning of the phrase? In 1786 the British parliament was debating the level of excise on whisky, and Burns' poem was addressed to the 45 Scottish MPs at Westminster, asking them to stand up for Scotland's interests. In the poem he argued that it was the consumption of whisky which had made Scotland fight for her freedom in the past:

Let half-starv'd slaves in warmer skies
See future wines, rich-clust'ring rise;
Their lot auld Scotland ne'er envies'
But blythe and frisky,
She sees her freeborn, martial boys
Tak aff their whisky.

And in this poem whisky becomes an icon, a symbol of the Scottish national identity. Defence of the national drink by the Scottish MPs is portrayed as a defence of Scotland's national economic interests, against the English gin distillers, plotting to tax whisky out of business.

In what is possibly Burn's greatest poem and certainly his most famous, *Tam O' Shanter* he further attributes the waxing of courage to the consumption of whisky. Indeed, he clearly distinguishes between the courage brought about by the consumption of ale, and that superior courage coming from whisky drinking:

Inspiring bold John Barleycorn!
What dangers thou canst make us scorn!
Wi' tippeny, we fear nae evil;
Wi' usquebae we'll face the devil!

However, though on one level *Tam O' Shanter* is a hymn to conviviality and uncontrolled drinking, the moral of the tale is really one of 'responsible drinking.' As a consequence of his over-indulgence Tam is almost dragged off to hell by the witches he encounters in Alloway Kirk on his ride home. This is when he bawls out drunkenly 'Weel done, Cutty-sark!' at the sight of an especially attractive witch with a short, revealing skirt. Only by passing over water, and losing his mare's tail in the chase, does Tam escape. Burns concludes the poem with a warning:

> *Now, wha this tale o' truth shall read,*
> *Each man and mother's son takk heed;*
> *Whene'er to drink you are inclin'd*
> *Or cutty-sarks rin in your mind.*
> *Think! ye may buy your joys o'er dear;*
> *Remember Tam o' Shanter's mare.*

There was a more serious side to this in that Burns, though here and elsewhere advocating self-restraint in drinking, himself was unable to practise what he preached, and became increasingly alcohol-dependent with time. In *Drink and the Devil* he gives full vent to his self disgust:

> *Yestreen, alas! I was sae fu'*
> *I could but yisk and wink;* [5]
> *And now, this day, sair, sair I rue,*
> *The weary, weary drink.*

But Burns' drunken over-indulgence brought him shame as well as depression. His misbehaviour at social gatherings, often amongst ladies of standing, haunted him. In a letter of apology to Mrs Robert Riddel, he wrote after such a debauch:

[5] Yisk = hiccup

41

Madam,

I write you from the regions of Hell, amid the horrors of the damned., on account of my conduct yesternight under your roof. An intoxicated man is the vilest of beasts.

Regret! Remorse! Shame! Ye three hell hounds that ever dog my steps and bay at my heels, spare me! Spare me!

Forgive the offenses, and pity the perdition of, Madam, your humble slave,

R.B.

This contradiction in Burns is echoed in that, for much of the latter part of his life, he was actually an exciseman, or gauger, intent on suppressing the illegal alcohol trade, but unable to curb his own excessive use of the product.

Burns was the Ploughman Poet, a poor peasant farmer who failed to make ends meet from his pen, despite his fame. When struggling to make a living farming, he took up a part-time job as an exciseman at £50 a year. Given Burns' attitude to whisky it is possibly unsurprising that from time to time he was lax in the execution of his duties.

On one occasion Burns entered the howff of an old dame suspected of selling illicit whisky and asked for a dram and some bread and cheese. When he offered to pay, the crone replied the he owed 'Naething ava for the whisky, but saxpence for the bread and cheese.' Laughingly Burns told her 'Sin on, and fear not,' and left the house. On another occasion he apprehended a whisky smuggler with his cart, and the man so moved Burns with the story of his poverty that the exciseman gave him a pound instead of arresting him.

In 1794 Burns moved to Dumfries, where his wages rose to £70 a year, more than ever he made from his poetry. That his heart was not in his work as a gauger was shown by the fact that in Dumfries he wrote the poem *The Exciseman* which celebrates the devil running off with the exciseman to the delight of the local population. The move to Dumfries was good for Burns' income but bad for his drinking. Conviviality and alcohol were linked in Scotland at this time in a way that would make today's binge drinkers appear temperate. Every social occasion, from Halloween to markets and fairs, was marked by excess alcoholic consumption. These were periodic indulgences for the lower classes but in the genteel Dumfries society Burns now moved in, steady, heavy drinking was the norm. One commentator wrote:

> *The whole town tipples; there are club rooms in every lane; the flow of drink is perpetual, the system of soaking knows no season. All classes drink – the schoolmaster, the curate, the publican and sinner, the tax gatherer, the exciseman, and the half-pay officer.*

Unable to resist such temptation Burns' addiction grew. In January 1796 after a visit to his favourite Globe Tavern, Burns fell asleep in the snow on the way home, catching a severe chill and rheumatic fever which was to contribute to his death later in that year – at the age of 37.

Burns wrote some of the finest love poems in any language, yet his treatment of women, who found him irresistible, was dreadful. He also wrote some of the best drinking songs ever, praising whisky in these above all other drink, but he was unable to enjoy the *craitur* without excess. Rabbie was a rogue, but he was aware of his flaws, of which women and drink were the main, and he hoped that, 'Whatever may be my failings, may they ever be those of a generous heart and an independent mind.' Indeed, they were. When we toast the 'Immortal Memory' of Scotland's National Bard with the country's national drink, let us note that he would have written many more wonderful songs had he used whisky as his servant, rather than as his master.

7 Whisky's Awa: The Rise and Fall of the Temperance Movement in Scotland

CURRENT DEBATES ON 'responsible drinking' and on the cost and availability of alcohol have a long pedigree. Scotland, the birthplace of modern industrial whisky making, also saw the birth of the first of the temperance movements and an examination of their rise and fall might be of use in informing the present discussion.

The beginnings of large-scale whisky commercial distilling in 1824 was facilitated by the reduction of the duty on spirits from 7s to 2s 6d (12.5p) a gallon – and a consequent reduction in the price of whisky. Consumption of the *craitur* in Scotland increased from about two million gallons in 1822 to approaching seven million in 1829, accompanied by a consequent increase in drunkenness. For example, in Glasgow from 1871-4 some 125,000 people were arrested as 'drunk and incapable'. Many people felt Something Had To Be Done.

Intemperance was an accepted part of upper-class Scottish society, but it had generally been conducted behind domestic doors or in private drinking clubs. The new urban working-class drunkenness on the other hand was manifested in public. Many early reformers were motivated by humanitarian impulses, but also by the fact that they felt the increasingly industrial society would be put at risk by work-men drinking, and that the middle classes would be taxed to pay the poor rates necessary to maintain the indigent drunken populace. From the outset the alcohol reformers target was the drink of the working man – and especially, their target was whisky. One sceptic commented that the rage against drunkenness was an 'artful combination of the upper classes against the toiling portion of the community by keeping back whisky from the common people.'

The first temperance society in the world was set up in Maryhill, then a village just outside Glasgow, by James Dunlop. This movement's target was whisky (and other spirits), and not the wine drunk domestically by the middle and upper classes, which was assumed to be 'nutritious'. Dunlop was aided in his work by the millionaire Glasgow printer and bible publisher William Collins, who did not endear himself to working men by arguing that they should only drink water. Collins' money funded hundreds of tracts and the issuance of the Temperance Society Record. Collins was an evangelical Christian who believed that drink was the cause of poverty, and of irreligion.

The early temperance movement was heavily religiously inspired. In 1842 an Irish priest, Theobald Mathew, led a procession of 50,000 people to Glasgow Green, where an estimated 80% of them signed a pledge to abstain from alcohol (though presumably not communion wine). Soon a whole range of societies burst into existence some advocating temperance (ie. a selective and moderate alcohol consumption) others increasingly becoming supporters of teetotalism, that is abstaining from all alcohol consumption, and still others going as far as prohibitionism, that is the banning of all production and sale of alcoholic drink.

In the Victorian period and well into the 20th century this now almost forgotten crusade against alcohol was a mass movement which had a great influence on politics. Christian groups continued to wage the campaign against the 'demon drink', greatly strengthened when the Salvation Army arrived in Scotland in 1879, with its lively open-air meetings and anti-alcohol message. But many other organisations rejected the simplistic view of drink causing poverty and argued rather that it was the other way round. The exploited working man had no hope and no escape except into drunkenness, and tackling poverty would lead to more success in combating alcohol abuse.

Movements such as the Independent Order of Rechabites waged temperance campaigns accompanied by the whole paraphernalia of uniforms and regalia that would provide colour in dull lives. The Rechabites were also a Friendly Society in the pre-welfare-state days, offering care for sickness and other benefits to those who practised temperance, and the loss of these if members lapsed. The Good Templars was another organisation which combined friend-

ly society benefits with ritual and colour often inspired by
Freemasonry, along with social activities and outings. It
soon had a Scottish membership of 80,000, including one
branch in Airdrie boasting over 4,000 members. The Band
of Hope was an abstinence organisation, this time aimed at
children and set up by William Quarrier, who established
orphan homes.

The combined pressure of all these organisations began
to bear legislative fruit. In 1853 a Licensing Act closed pubs
on Sundays and at 11pm on weekdays, and the increasing
power of the anti-drink lobby meant that it became difficult
to get new licences. Women and children were also selec-
tively banned from public houses. In Glasgow by the later
19th century under a succession of provosts including
William Collins Jnr, alcohol was forbidden on council
premises – a ban that lasted until 1960, and Collins made it
clear that had the law of the land allowed, he would have
introduced prohibition in Glasgow. This pressure reached
its culmination in 1913 when the Temperance (Scotland)
Act became law, allowing for local plebiscites on the sale of
alcohol. In the 1920s over 40 areas in Scotland voted to
become 'dry' – but as these were mainly middle-class resi-
dential areas, the effect was limited.

Initially many working-class reformers and trades union-
ists opposed the temperance movement as middle-class
busybodies. But as the 19th century progressed the Labour

movement more and more adopted the crusaders' message against drink, which its leaders saw, not as the cause of working-class poverty, but as something which made it worse – and whose effects made working men less able to hear the socialist message of hope. Thus many of the early leaders of the Labour movement in Scotland such as Keir Hardie and John Maclean, were teetotal. The Co-operative movement – where working-class womens' influence was strong – was especially down on drink, and it was not until 1958 that any of the branches of the SCWS were permitted to sell alcohol.

This alliance between Labour and temperance had a dramatic outcome in Dundee, where the radical socialist and prohibitionist Edwin Scrymgeour was elected to parliament in 1922 – beating Winston Churchill. While the men of Dundee might have been voting for Scrymgeour's firebrand socialism, the women were supporting him for his plans to outlaw the manufacture of alcohol altogether; and alcohol for the working man still meant largely whisky in those days. Scrymgeour introduced his Prohibitionist Bill to parliament in 1923 where it failed by 335 to 14.

The failure of this one attempt to introduce prohibition into Britain was soon followed by its introduction into the United States of America. The disastrous consequences of this measure, with its massive increase in racketeering and its limited effect on alcohol consumption, meant that the

ideas of prohibition were discredited, and the issue dropped
from the political agenda. Trying to prohibit the production of alcohol is today seen as a hopeless cause, and, while
individuals might themselves 'Take the Pledge', few of them
nowadays would hope to persuade the majority of their fel-
lows to do the same. Ironically though, today's 'sensible
drinking' mantra is quite close to that of the early temperance reformers, before they moved towards their less toler-
ant teetotal and prohibitionist positions.

8 Lewis Whisky and the Case
of the Illicit Still

AT ABHAINN DEARG by Uig Bay on the Isle of Lewis, which location I personally hold to be the most beautiful place on earth, there was recently established the first legal distillery to operate on the Isle of Lewis for at least a century and a half. In a former fish-bait shed the 'Spirit of Lewis' is lovingly produced from local barley. What the distillery's owners did not anticipate was that the enthusiasm for their enterprise would extend so far as to their finding an illicit still from the 1950s dumped outside the shed one morning, donated anonymously by someone who clearly wanted their project to succeed.

The brief Lewis experiment with legal whisky distilling had ended by the 1860s, but that illicit still is 'proof' that the island's distilling tradition had carried on many years after most people had assumed it had vanished. The distillation of spirits has as long a history in the Outer Isles as it does elsewhere in Scotland. When Martin Martin visited Lewis in about 1695, he commented:

Their plenty of corn was such as disposed the natives to brew several sorts of liquors, as common usquebaugh, another called trestarig, id est, aqua-vitae, three times distilled, which is strong and hot, a third sort is four times distilled, and this by the natives is called usqubaugh-baul ... two spoonfulls of this last liquor is a sufficient dose; and if any man exceed this, it would presently stop his breath and endanger his life.

Martin added that, 'The trestarig and usquebaugh-baul are both made of oats' and the use of oats for distilling is confirmed by the Revd JL Buchanan who visited Lewis a century later and noted that oats and not barley was the favoured grain. However by the mid-18th century natural selection had 'created' whisky as we now know it, as opposed to the various other spirits and cordials, and barley was being used for whisky distillation in Lewis just as elsewhere. The drink's popularity grew amongst the townspeople of Stornoway, whose richer inhabitants were reported to be partly paying their maidservants' wages in whisky – at the rate of a wine glass each morning! Its popularity also began to replace that of ale amongst the country people, but the main reason for domestic distillation was not the legally permitted one of personal consumption, but that of 'paying' the rent.

In the century before 1840, the main method a Lewis peasant had of getting money to pay his rent was to convert a part of his crop to whisky, sell it, and hand the money gained over to the landlord. In 1833 the minister of Stornoway Parish stated in the *New Statistical Account* that,

Formerly when each tenant was allowed to convert the produce of his little lot into usquebaugh, or tres-tarig, that is thrice distilled, it

was solely to pay his rent, – illicit distillation had not the same dete-riorating effect here on the morals of the people as on the mainland.

Leaving the second part of the reverend gentleman's asser-tion aside for the moment, the first is undoubtedly accurate, and confirmed by other accounts which all state that the distilling was small-scale, never attaining the commercial magnitude of operations taking place at the same time, for example, on mainland areas like Donside in Aberdeenshire.

The main reason for this would appear to be, possibly, not only the superior moral quality of the Lewis popula-tion, but simply, lack of opportunity. Even more so than in remote mainland Highland areas, the market available for mass-produced illicit whisky was just not there; the popula-tion of the whole of the Outer Isles in 1800 was less than 10,000, and the logistics of getting any large amounts of ille-gally produced whisky off the island and to distant cus-tomers was simply beyond the capability and probably even the imagination of the largely monoglot and un-entrepre-neurial Gaelic peasants of Lewis, moral though they undoubtedly were.

The owners of Lewis at this time were the Mackenzies of Seaforth, who encouraged and supported this illegal distil-lation, as a means of ensuring their rents were paid. Not only that, they appear to have negotiated a deal with the excise that allowed Lewis crofters the right to produce and sell more than they personally consumed. In a letter to the treasury dated 1824 (a year after the total overhaul of the distilling legislation), Stewart Mackenzie protested that this right had been withdrawn, and the harassment of the distillation subsequently was making it difficult for the tenants to pay, and Mackenzie to collect, their rents. [6]

The late 1820s saw an increase in the efforts of the excisemen, which met with growing success with the arrests of crofters in Back, Coll, Barvas Habost, South Lochs, Shawbost and South Bragar, along with subsequent fines and imprisonment. Crofters retreated from the moors to remote caves. *Gheodha Beuc* (Noisy Cave) at the Butt of Lewis and *Geodha Thogallaich* (Brewing Cave) in Tolsta became the last refuges of the distillers though even they were not safe from small boats set into the narrow inlets from the revenue cutters. The effect on living standards of the suppression of illicit distilling was outlined by the then estate factor John Munro Mackenzie in 1851, ' ... when times changed and whisky could no longer be made, those who did not change their occupation and become fishermen are now very ill off.'

[6] Extract from Mackenzie of Seaforth's letter to the Treasury in 1824. In it he asked for permission to establish a distillery at Stornoway, in order to end what he called, 'The wicked and disastrous system of vexation and fines, and all the frauds and oppression caused by the excise system, which the ignorance and prejudice of the poor wretched tenantry would never view in any other way, recollecting or acting upon the knowledge that *until a very short period, their landlord, by a very small pecuniary compromise with the Government, purchased for them a special immunity for carrying on illicit distillation, by farming the excise.*' (Italicised emphasis is the author's). From Donald MacDonald, *Lewis* (2004 edn) p190. MacDonald states that 'illicit distillation practically ceased' in Lewis by the 1840s.

Out of this dilemma came the first experiment with legal distillation in Lewis. Stewart Mackenzie himself set up a legal distillery, buy his tenants' surplus grain off them (receiving the money back as rent!) and then turn that peasant produce into a profitable distilling enterprise. Lewis had plenty of water, plenty of fuel (peat) and surplus barley ... it seemed a good idea at the time, and Mackenzie poured the considerable sum of £14,000 into the venture. By 1833 the minister at Stornoway could write that amongst the 'modern' buildings in the town:

> *There is also a distillery on a grand scale, with coppers of large diameter, furnaces, vats, coolers, flake-stands under a running stream; also a very large malt barn and mill.*

The works were situated at the Shoe Burn which lies in the grounds of the present Lewis Castle. One Mr Macnee was engaged as the chief distiller and became a well-liked fellow in the town, earning the nickname Thomas Mhor. This might have been due to the size of the drams he dispensed to the townspeople and sailors who bought whisky at the distillery. He apparently was giving measures greater than they had paid for! Efforts were made to supply the Glasgow market with the product, and there was even some discussion of appointing a London agent, but most of the whisky appears to have met the local demand of townsfolk and passing sailors in Stornoway.

It is often stated, and was recently re-affirmed in the *Stornoway Gazette*, that the Shoeburn Distillery closed just before or just after the Mathesons bought Lewis in 1844. However a perusal of the diary of the estate chamberlain, or factor, John Munro Mackenzie, from 1851, shows that this was not the case, and in fact expansion appears to have been the keynote. In March 1851 he recorded his search along the Laxdale River with a view to 'fixing the site of Mill dam and lead [lade] for Distillery'.

Construction duly commenced and by December Mackenzie was able to note with satisfaction that the work was complete and that he had, 'Remained at the Distillery all day seeing the men paid & arranged various matters with foremen.' One of the men he mentions being the above-mentioned chief distiller Mr Macnee. It is this clear that Shoeburn Distillery continued in operation well into the 1850s, contrary to received opinion, and that Matheson, a convinced temperance advocate, continued to produce and profit from whisky distillation at Stornoway for at least a decade after he purchased the island. One source gives 1857 as the date Matheson demolished the works and replaced it with stables. Lewis was not to become another Islay ... possibly that local market was just too small and Stornoway just too far away from larger centres of demand (though the Orkney distilleries of this period flourished) for Shoeburn to survive.

Matheson, the Christian evangelical teetotaller, had made his fortune supplying the Chinese market with opium from India and in the process turned a large proportion of China's population into drug addicts; in addition it lead to that country's bankruptcy. Matheson's duplicitous nature was also shown in that while continuing to produce legal whisky, at the same time he tightened the screw against illicit distilling. His factor wrote clauses into tenants' leases stipulating that the penalty for distillation of any kind was eviction.

Other factors possibly helped to strangle illicit distillation in Lewis. The island was fortunate – or unfortunate – in that the two excise revenue cutters which patrolled the whole Minch and Atlantic seaboards, pursuing smugglers and distillers, were based at Stornoway. Then there was the rise in the power of the Free Kirk from the 1840s on the island, which organisation would take a less latitudinarian approach to all things illicit – including illicit distilling – than their Church of Scotland predecessors, some of whom appear to have been involved in smuggling. (The Barvas minister was denounced to the gaugers in the 1790s for running an illicit still). Finally, given the small local demand and inability to meet the wider mainland demand, there was little financial incentive, but a great risk, in illicit distillation.

And so by 1850, the tradition of the illegal pot still had died out on Lewis. Maybe there was drinking going in the numberless moorland bothans for a century-and-a-half afterwards, but all due tax on the *craitur* imbibed had been paid ... so goes the conventional wisdom. But then, where did that copper kettle left outside Abhainn Dearg come from? Rather than having given up illicit distillation, were the Lewis folk just smart enough to have avoided detection? The answer lies hidden in the trackless, misty moors of Eilean Fraoch.

9 The Last Distiller Had the Last Laugh

THOUGH DOUBTLESS THE odd sma' still might yet be found in remote areas of the West Highlands, the last illicit distiller on a scale large enough to provide his main income must have been Hamish *Dhubh* Macrae of Monar, who retired from his calling a century ago. He and his father had outwitted the excisemen for over 60 years, and even in finally giving up his trade, Hamish had the last laugh.

Hamish's father Alasdair and his wife had originally come to Loch Monar from Kintail in the 1840s. Monar is and was one of the remotest parts of the Scottish mainland, accessible only by drove roads and bridle paths. Alasdair built a house on an island at the western end of Loch Monar, and by having the 'lum reekin' before he was challenged, gained squatter's rights. He also built a causeway to connect the little fortress to the mainland. But the fire in his house was not the only one Alasdair lit.

It seems that the Macraes had come deliberately to Monar to engage in the illicit production of whisky. Monar was 40 miles, and hard miles at that, from the nearest gauger's office in Dingwall. Alasdair originally had bothies at a place called Cosaig at the lochside, but when he suffered the indignity of being arrested by the gaugers and taken to

Dingwall for trial, he vowed never to be captured again, and to improve the concealment of his trade.

He rebuilt his stills high on the side of a mountain overlooking Loch Monar, called Meall Mor, and here Hamish his son was apprenticed to the trade by being posted with a spyglass to keep a lookout for the excisemen coming up the glen. On one occasion, when snow fell and Hamish did not want footsteps to reveal the location of the stills, he stayed for several cold and hungry days on the bothy, high on Meall Mor, until the snow melted.

Though Alasdair, and Hamish after him, grew a few potatoes and indulged in a spot of poaching his main income was from the whisky; the winter months were given over to distillation, and the summer ones to distribution. There were customers in the area; the local gamekeepers and shepherds living in Glen Strathfarrar, east of Loch Monar supplied outlets as did passing drovers and tinkers, more numerous in those days. But the Macraes also sold to local hostelries in the district, and even visited fairs at Dingwall and elsewhere, selling *The Pait Blend* under the noses of the authorities. The whisky was named after a knoll, *Pait* (Gaelic: a hump) just opposite their island home.

Alasdair lived to the ripe old age of 97, and both he and his wife were carried back in their coffins for burial to the graveyard on Loch Duich in Kintail, by rough roads amounting to over 20 miles. The mountaineer, Revd AE

Robertson, who took a photograph of Hamish and Mairi about 1905, knew the Macraes well and was told the story of their mother's funeral. The porters were well supplied with illicit whisky that day, and one of them commented of Alasdair's wife that 'She was a big heavy woman too' – adding that they required many stops for refreshment. One of these stops nearly led to a disaster, when the over-refreshed porters subsequently found themselves in Kintail – without the coffin – and had to return many weary miles to retrieve it.

Hamish carried on the good work after his father's death. He was a colourful character, considering himself the equal of any, refusing to speak anything but Gaelic, and donning full Highland dress to visit the laird, Captain Stirling, at Pait Lodge (where a bottle reputedly changed hands) on Sundays. He and his sister Mairi were actually born at Monar and spent their entire lives there. Another brother, Alexander, emigrated to New Zealand and became part of an illicit whisky distilling dynasty in Southland (see Chapter 10).

Local people connived with the Macraes in the production of their whisky, sending runners ahead to warn them that the excisemen were on their way. On one occasion the gaugers were welcomed into a house in Strathfarrar, and entertained while news of their arrival was sent ahead. In the house the gaugers over-indulged in whisky (possibly Hamish's own) and felt so hungover the next day that they abandoned their search and returned to Dingwall empty-handed and sorry-headed.

But by the early 1900s there were fewer illicit distillers to chase, and the noose was tightening, making it more difficult for Hamish to live off his trade. And he was getting old, and had also heard the wonderful news that Lloyd George had introduced old-age pensions. Captain Stirling prevailed upon Hamish to give the distilling up. But Hamish turned even his retirement to good use. While at a fair in Beauly he approached a couple of excisemen and informed them, that if he could receive the £5 reward, he would show them the location of some illicit stills. He then led the guagers to his own bothies, and pocketed the reward, while they delightedly took away the stills for destruction. The ruins of the bothies are still there on Meall Mor for those who search, but the Macraes' island home was sadly submerged by the building of the Monar dam in 1959, and the raising of the water level.

Jamie and his sister retired to the old folks' home at Kilmorack, and on their deaths were also taken back to Kintail for burial beside their parents – though this time they were transported by road, not carried on foot as their parents had been. The Macraes of Monar have passed into history and *The Pait Blend* into folklore, its famed taste a fond memory ... unless there is still a bottle lying beneath the waters of Loch Monar?

10 New Zealand Moonshine: The Hokonui Brand

MARY McRAE SAILED for New Zealand on the emigrant ship The *Hydaspes* in 1872. Recently widowed, she took with her her four sons and three daughters, and her memories of her 45 hard years in Kintail, the MacRae heartland. She also took with her a wooden box marked 'Household Goods', which contained one of the most essential household items in Kintail at that time. This was a fine copper and brass whisky still, which was to have a colourful history once it was reassembled on her new holding in the Hokonui hills of Southland in New Zealand's South Island.

She left behind in Kintail a conviction for illegal distilling, which had attracted to her – or rather to her son Duncan – a massive £650 fine, with an additional £150 for non-appearance at court, for operating a still on Kishorn island in Kintail. Mary's husband had died the year before, and possibly dire economic necessity had driven her to illicit distilling to support her large family, as it did many others. There is no record of the fine being paid before Mary left Scotland, indeed such a sum would have been impossible for a poor Highland crofter to find.

The McRaes settled in the Southland district which was heavily populated by Scots, particularly Scots Highlanders, with many hundreds from Kintail itself. The locals still universally spoke Gaelic, played the classical bagpipe (*piobaireachd*), and had a taste for whisky – which was very expensive if imported. There existed a local hooch produced from the Cabbage Tree, but this deadly brew was more of a rum than a whisky, and Mary soon found a ready demand for her *craitur* when she started distilling again with her sons. At events in the local Celtic Society Hall and as far away as Invercargill at the Caledonian Sports Society's Games, the Hokonui brand soon found a market.

This was still frontier time in Southland, and the authorities could only make limited efforts to control illicit stills, of which there were many besides Mary's. On one occasion officers came to her cabin and listened at the window to the conversation for clues – as the talk inside was all in Gaelic, they went away as mystified as when they had come. On another occasion the customs officers might have been more lucky, had Mary (now known as the *cailleach*) not sat down over a whisky barrel, covering it with her skirt and remaining seated while the exciseman made his search.

Mary died in 1911 at the ripe old age of 92, and she attributed her lifelong good health to a daily dose of her own dram. In the years after the First World War, however, the frontier epoch had passed away and the increasingly resourceful authorities took a more active role in eradicating illegal whisky distilling in Southland, where many stills, including Mary's own, were still in operation. One law enforcement official said, 'Southland is absolutely notorious for the distillation of whisky, which everyone knows had been carried on here for over fifty years.'

The first successful prosecution was in 1924, when Alex Chisholm and Alexander McRae were fined $200NZ (£100). Then in 1928 came the Awarua case, when another illicit still was found and smashed, and a similar fine imposed to the case four years previously. But the *cailleach*'s own still was still bubbling away merrily. One Duncan 'Piper' McRae (no relation) had married the *cailleach*'s daughter and he carried on the production of whisky with her still, which then passed through further generations of the family. By 1928 intermarriage had brought it into the hands of Duncan Stuart, who operated the still at Otapiri Gorge.

Stuart was producing on a large scale, and it was his main employment. According to the Customs Department, he was making 10 gallons of whisky a month, representing a loss in customs revenue of $1260 a year. Selling the whisky at $4 a gallon brought him $10 – the equivalent of £5 a week – a tidy income in the 1920s. A massive fine of $1000 and confiscation of the still meant an end to the life of the equipment which had operated in Southland for almost 60 years – and for an untold number of years in Kintail before that. However there was one more chapter in the Southland whisky saga before it became history.

One of the problems facing excisemen in Southland was the thick cover of bush. This meant that smoke from the stills became dispersed through the leaf canopy and difficult to spot. Knowing there were stills operating in the Dunsdale area of Southland, the exisemen came up with a novel idea – aerial surveillance, by which they might hope to discern the dispersing clouds of smoke.

John Smith was the instructor with Southland Aero Club, and the Collector of Customs chartered him and his Gypsy Moth in 1934 to overfly the bush around Dunsdale where another family of McRaes, William, father and son, were under suspicion. Now this family of McRaes had a reputation. Back in the 1890s John McRae, also a whisky-maker had been accused of murder in a very murky case involving whisky and women. Though he had been acquitted here was clearly a family not to meddle with. Smith later recalled how he earned his fee, but avoided any personal problems.

> He (the customs official) *went straight up to the wall map and pointed out the spot where the still was set up and said 'You know what to do.' I knew what would happen if I flew over that place, it would be a bullet first and questions afterwards. There was a west wind blowing and I took the collector all around the Hokonuis till the turbulence made him ill, but I never went anywhere near that still.*

Eventually though, the excisemen found the still, which McRae had set up just outside his farm on Maori

Reservation land. When challenged he said, 'It if is outside my boundaries, I would not know anything about it.' Indeed, the evidence against the McRaes was mainly circumstantial, and when brought to court they were discharged by the jury. The police however, wrecked the still and this was really the end of the 60 or more years of Hokonui hooch.

It is just a pity that visitors cannot taste it any more, as reports of consumers in the past testify to its excellence. 'It was just like whisky', said one witness at a court case asked to describe its taste, and what higher praise could there be?